Helen Exley Giftbooks
for the most thoughtful gifts of all

OTHER BOOKS IN THIS SERIES:
For a wonderful Mother A book to make your own
For a wonderful Grandmother A book to make your own
For a real Friend A book to make your own
A Girl's Journal A personal notebook and keepsake
Cats A book to make your own
Teddy Bears A book to make your own
Inspirations A book to make your own
A Gardener's Journal A book to make your own
OTHER HELEN EXLEY GIFTBOOKS
FOR WOMEN:
In Celebration of Women
Woman to Woman
The Best of Women's Quotations
Men! by women
Ms Murphy's Law

Published in hardback 1990. Published in softcover 2001.
Copyright © Helen Exley 1990, 2001
Selection © Helen Exley 1990, 2001
The moral right of the author has been asserted.

12 11 10 9 8 7 6 5 4 3

ISBN 1-86187-219-4

Selection and design by Helen Exley
Illustrated by Juliette Clarke
Printed in China

Exley Publications Ltd, 16 Chalk Hill, Watford, Herts, WD1 4BN, UK.
Exley Publications LLC, 232 Madison Avenue, Suite 1409, NY 10016, USA.

Acknowledgements: The publishers are grateful for permission to reproduce copyright material. Whilst every reasonable effort has been made to trace copyright holders, we would be pleased to hear from any not here acknowledged. Anne Morrow Lindbergh: From *Gift From The Sea*. Reprinted with permission.

A Woman's
Journal

A personal notebook and keepsake

A HELEN EXLEY GIFTBOOK

EXLEY
NEW YORK • WATFORD, UK

What is better than gold?
  Jasper.
What is better than jasper?
  Wisdom.
What is better than wisdom?
  Women.
And what is better than a good woman?
  Nothing.

GEOFFREY CHAUCER (1340–1400)

For women there are,
undoubtedly,
great difficulties in the path,
but so much the more
to overcome.
First, no woman should say,
"I am but a woman!"
But a woman! What more
can you ask to be?

MARIA MITCHELL
(1818-1889)

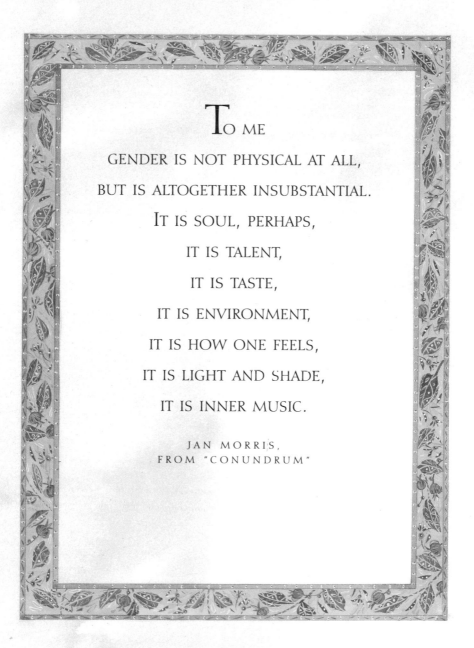

To me
GENDER IS NOT PHYSICAL AT ALL,
BUT IS ALTOGETHER INSUBSTANTIAL.
IT IS SOUL, PERHAPS,
IT IS TALENT,
IT IS TASTE,
IT IS ENVIRONMENT,
IT IS HOW ONE FEELS,
IT IS LIGHT AND SHADE,
IT IS INNER MUSIC.

JAN MORRIS,
FROM "CONUNDRUM"

Traditionally we are taught, and instinctively we long,

to give where it is needed – and immediately.

Eternally, woman spills herself away in driblets to the thirsty,

seldom being allowed the time, the quiet, the peace,

to let the pitcher fill up to the brim.

ANNE MORROW LINDBERGH, B.1906,
FROM "GIFT FROM THE SEA"

$\mathcal{I}$n my younger days, when I was pained
by the half-educated, loose and inaccurate
ways women had, I used to say,
"How much women need exact science."
But since I have known some workers
in science, I have now said,
"How much science needs women."

MARIA MITCHELL (1818-1889)

*ℬeing a woman
is of special interest
only to aspiring
male transsexuals.
To actual women,
it is simply a good excuse
not to play football.*

FRAN LEBOWITZ, B.1950

*Above the titles
of wife and mother,
which,
although dear,
are transitory and
accidental,
there is the title
human being,
which precedes and
outranks every other.*

MARY ASHTON LIVERMORE
(c . 1 8 2 0 - 1 9 0 5)

It is <u>new</u> for women to be making history
– not just a few queens,
empresses or exceptional geniuses,
but hundreds, thousands,
millions of women now entering history,
knowing we have made history
– by changing our own lives.

BETTY FRIEDAN, B.1921,
FROM "IT CHANGED MY LIFE"

I don't know why it should
surprise people women are so tough.
What I do is probably not as tough
as [being] a single mother,
raising two kids and paying rent or a mortgage.

LIBBY RIDDLES, SLED-DOG RACE WINNER

*At present,
we insist that a woman
be treated just the same
as a man.
Are we sure we want to be treated
as most men are
in our society?
Or do both sexes deserve
something better?*

KAY KEESHAN HAMOD,
FROM "WORKING IT OUT"

*What a circus act we women perform
every day of our lives. It puts the trapeze artist
to shame. Look at us. We run a tight rope daily,
balancing a pile of books on the head.
Baby-carriage, parasol, kitchen chair, still under control.
Steady now!*

ANNE MORROW LINDBERGH, B.1906,
FROM "GIFT FROM THE SEA"

$\mathcal{W}$omen... often... need to return to their past,
to the women who were part of that past,
to girlhood when a self existed that was individual
and singular, defined neither by men,
nor children, nor home, almost as though with
the layers of roles and responsibilities they have
covered over a real person and must now peel back
those layers and reclaim the self that was just
emerging in adolescence.

MARY HELEN WASHINGTON

... each woman

is far from average

in the daily heroics of her life,

even though she may never receive

a moment's recognition in history.

INTRODUCTION TO
"WOMEN & WORK"

Everything that gives birth is female.
When men begin to understand the relationships of the universe
that women have always known,
the world will begin to change for the better.

LORRAINE CANOE (MOHAWK)

I don't believe
make-up and the right
hairstyle alone can
make a woman
beautiful.
The most radiant
woman in the room
is the one most full of
life and experience.

SHARON STONE

A̲LL WOMEN

HAVE A SACRED OBLIGATION

TO EACH OTHER

IRRESPECTIVE OF CLASS

OR CONDITIONS OF WORK.

VIDA GOLDSTEIN

I don't mind
being in
a man's world
so long as
I can be
a woman in it.

MARILYN MONROE
(1926-1962)

It would be a thousand pities if women wrote like men,
or lived like men, or looked like men,
for if two sexes are quite inadequate,
considering the vastness and variety of the world,
how should we manage with one only?

VIRGINIA WOOLF (1882-1941)

Being nice should <u>never</u> be perceived as being weak.
It's not a sign of weakness, it's a sign of courtesy, manners,
grace, a woman's ability to make everyone... feel at home,
and it should never be construed as weakness....

BENAZIR BHUTTO, B.1953

One of the wonderful
things about women, which
I don't think many social
anthropologists have fully
understood, is that we are
bonded by shared
experiences....

ANITA RODDICK, B.1943,
FROM "BODY AND SOUL"

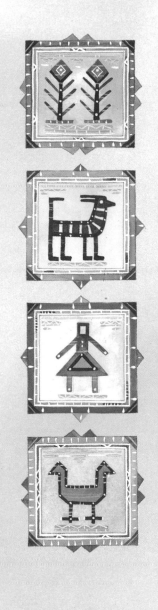

I THINK THE KEY IS FOR WOMEN
NOT TO SET ANY LIMITS.

MARTINA NAVRATILOVA, B.1956

Very often,

men are pursuing some

fantasy of school,

or their fathers,

or their nation.

Women are slightly

more rooted in themselves.

That's not to say they're

more introspective,

but they just have

a presence;

they've had to.

JOAN BAKEWELL, B.1933

*Womankind holds at its heart
the understanding that love, not power,
ensures the continuance of life.
Each woman holds the hope of reconciliation,
of sanity, of peace, of strength in kindness,
of humankind discovering it is one family.*

PAM BROWN, B.1928

*W*omen never have an half-hour in all their lives
(excepting before or after anybody is up in the house)
that they can call their own,
without fear of offending or of hurting someone.
Why do people sit up so late, or, more rarely, get up so early?
Not because the day is not long enough,
but because they have "no time in the day to themselves."

FLORENCE NIGHTINGALE (1820-1910),
FROM "CASSANDRA"

I BELIEVE THAT WHAT A WOMAN RESENTS
IS NOT SO MUCH GIVING HERSELF IN PIECES
AS GIVING HERSELF PURPOSELESSLY.

ANNE MORROW LINDBERGH, B.1906

WE WOMEN SUFFRAGISTS
HAVE A GREAT MISSION —
THE GREATEST MISSION THE
WORLD HAS EVER KNOWN.
IT IS TO FREE
HALF THE HUMAN RACE,
AND THROUGH THAT REASON
TO SAVE THE REST.

EMMELINE PANKHURST
(1857-1928)

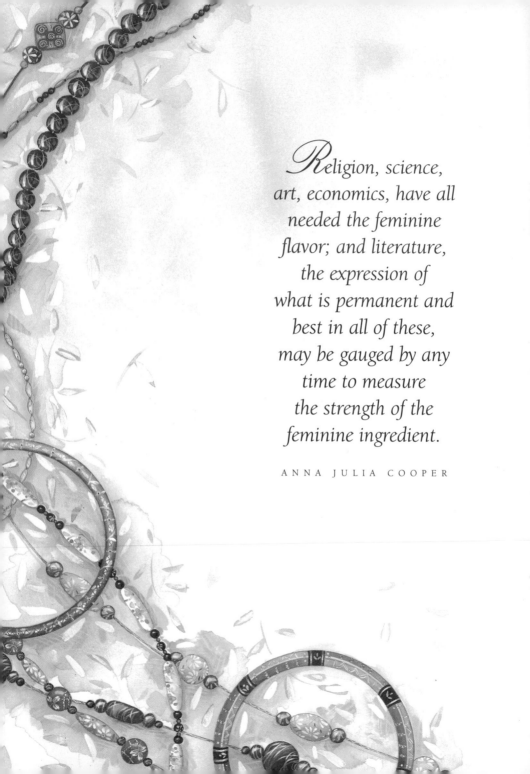

*Religion, science,
art, economics, have all
needed the feminine
flavor; and literature,
the expression of
what is permanent and
best in all of these,
may be gauged by any
time to measure
the strength of the
feminine ingredient.*

ANNA JULIA COOPER

T HE GOLDEN RULE
WORKS FOR MEN AS WRITTEN,
BUT FOR WOMEN IT SHOULD GO THE OTHER WAY AROUND.
WE NEED TO DO UNTO OURSELVES
AS WE DO UNTO OTHERS.

GLORIA STEINEM, B.1934

*For the sake of the sons –
and even for the sons'
future wives – a woman must
keep a part of her mind and
heart entirely for herself.
Every family is better off with
a wife and mother
who can astonish and
occasionally bewilder.*

PAM BROWN, B.1928

*W*omen speak because they wish to speak,
whereas a man speaks only when driven
to speech by something outside himself
– like, for instance,
he can't find any clean socks.

JEAN KERR

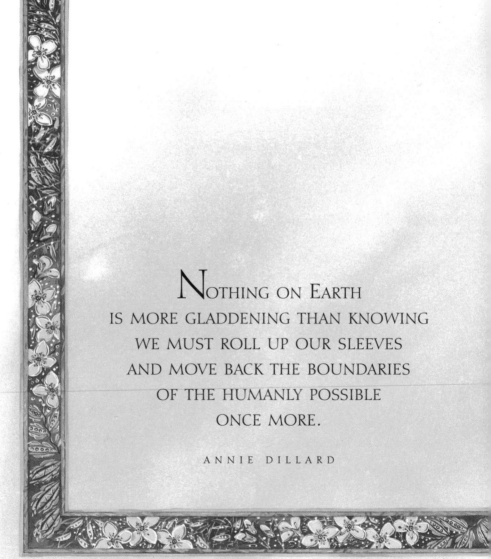

NOTHING ON EARTH
IS MORE GLADDENING THAN KNOWING
WE MUST ROLL UP OUR SLEEVES
AND MOVE BACK THE BOUNDARIES
OF THE HUMANLY POSSIBLE
ONCE MORE.

ANNIE DILLARD

$\mathcal{T}$he people I'm furious with
are the women's liberationists.
They keep getting up on soap boxes
and proclaiming that women are brighter than men.
It's true but it should be kept quiet
or it ruins the whole racket.

ANITA LOOS, B.1893

Even today when we extol the virtues
of our mamas, most often it's
a litany of hard work,
of what she did without and what she gave
– never what she took or expected
or demanded as her due.

MARCIA ANN GILLESPIE

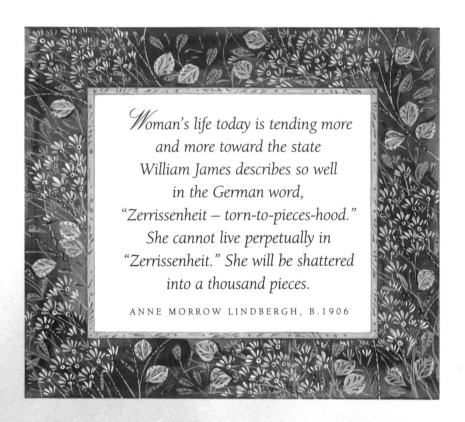

Woman's life today is tending more
and more toward the state
William James describes so well
in the German word,
"Zerrissenheit – torn-to-pieces-hood."
She cannot live perpetually in
"Zerrissenheit." She will be shattered
into a thousand pieces.

ANNE MORROW LINDBERGH, B.1906

WE REJECT PEDESTALS,
QUEENHOOD,
AND WALKING TEN PACES BEHIND.
TO BE RECOGNIZED AS HUMAN,
LEVELLY HUMAN,
IS ENOUGH.

COMBAHEE RIVER COLLECTIVE

Mothering/nurturing is a vital force and process establishing relationships throughout the universe. Exploring and analyzing the nature of all components involved in a nurturing activity puts one in touch with life extending itself. This is the feminine presence. The earth is woman.

BERNICE J. REAGON

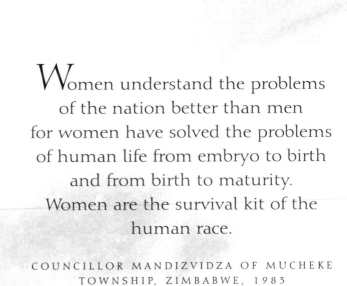

Women understand the problems
of the nation better than men
for women have solved the problems
of human life from embryo to birth
and from birth to maturity.
Women are the survival kit of the
human race.

COUNCILLOR MANDIZVIDZA OF MUCHEKE
TOWNSHIP, ZIMBABWE, 1983

WOMEN ONCE KNEW THEIR PLACE

– AND SO DO WE.

OUR HOME IS THE UNIVERSE.

OUR TASK IS ANYTHING WE SET OUR MINDS AND HEARTS TO.

MAYA V. PATEL, B. 1943